PHIL FODEN

The Kid Who Loved Football - How a
Dreamer Became a Manchester City Star

(A BIOGRAPHY FOR KIDS)

Kelli E. Owens

Phil foden

Phil foden

Disclaimer

This book contains information that is solely meant to be

educational. Despite their best efforts to present accurate

and current information, the author and publisher disclaim all expressed and implied representations and

warranties regarding the availability, completeness, accuracy, reliability, suitability, or suitability of the content contained herein for any purpose. The publisher

and the author disclaim all responsibility for any loss or

harm, including without limitation, consequential or indirect loss or damage, or any loss or damage at all

resulting from lost profits or data resulting from using

this book.

TABLE OF CONTENTS

INTRODUCTION

Who is Phil Foden?

Phil Foden is a name that shines brightly in the world of football. Known for his exceptional talent, quick feet, and love for the game, Phil has captured the hearts of fans around the globe. But before he became the star we see today, Phil was just a boy with a dream, kicking a ball around the streets of Stockport, England. This is the story of how a young boy's passion, determination, and hard work turned his dreams into reality.

Phil foden

From the moment Phil could walk, he seemed
destined for football. Growing up in a close-knit
family, he spent countless hours playing with his
friends and dreaming of becoming a professional
footballer. His journey wasn't always easy, but
Phil's love for the game kept him going.
Whether it was practicing under the rain or
overcoming challenges, Phil's commitment to his
dream was unwavering.

At just eight years old, Phil joined Manchester
City's academy, one of the best football schools
in the world. He was smaller than some of the
other kids, but his skills and determination stood
out. Coaches and teammates quickly noticed that
Phil wasn't just another player; he had
something special. Through years of hard work
and dedication, Phil climbed the ranks,

eventually earning a spot on Manchester City's senior team.

Now, Phil Foden is not only a key player for Manchester City but also a proud representative of England on the international stage. His journey inspires kids everywhere, proving that with hard work, dreams can come true. This book will take you on an exciting journey through Phil's life—from his early days kicking a ball in his backyard to becoming one of the brightest stars in football today.

Phil's story isn't just about football; it's about believing in yourself, working hard, and never giving up on your dreams. Whether you love football or simply enjoy tales of determination and triumph, Phil Foden's story will inspire you to chase your own dreams with all your heart.

Phil foden

CHAPTER 1: GROWING UP IN STOCKPORT

Stockport, a town just outside Manchester in England, is where Phil Foden's incredible story began. Born on May 28, 2000, Phil grew up in a humble, close-knit family. His parents, Claire and Phil Sr., worked hard to provide for their children, teaching Phil the values of hard work, humility, and dedication. These early lessons would shape his journey to football stardom.

Phil's childhood in Stockport was filled with simple joys. Like many kids in the area, he loved spending time outdoors, playing with his friends in parks or on the quiet streets of his neighborhood. Football quickly became his favorite pastime. From a young age, it was clear that he had a natural talent for the game. Whether it was kicking a ball against a wall or organizing makeshift matches with local kids, Phil's love for football was unmatched.

A Family of Supporters

The Foden household was more than just a home—it was a place where dreams were nurtured. Phil's parents, though not wealthy, did everything they could to support their son's passion. They bought him football boots, drove him to local games, and cheered him on at every opportunity. His father, Phil Sr., shared Phil's love for Manchester City, and together, they would watch matches, dreaming of the day Phil might wear the team's iconic blue jersey.

Phil's sister also played a significant role in his life. As his biggest cheerleader, she supported him through his highs and lows, always encouraging him to chase his dreams. This strong family bond gave Phil the confidence to believe in himself and his abilities.

Early Signs of Greatness

Even as a little boy, Phil stood out. His teachers and neighbors noticed his extraordinary skills with a football. While most children played for fun, Phil played with purpose. He had an instinct for the game that was rare for someone so young. He could dribble past opponents effortlessly, and his ability to read the game was far beyond his years.

Despite his natural talent, Phil was not one to boast. He remained grounded and focused, always eager to improve. His humility and dedication earned him the admiration of his peers and coaches alike.

Stockport: A Football Town

Stockport is a town that breathes football. Local parks and fields are filled with aspiring players honing their skills, and the community is deeply passionate about the sport. Growing up in such an environment only fueled Phil's love for football. He spent countless hours practicing in local parks, often losing track of time because he was so immersed in the game.

The town's rich football culture also meant that young Phil was surrounded by role models and mentors who recognized his potential. They encouraged him to aim high and never give up on his dreams.

Dreams Begin to Take Shape

As Phil grew older, his love for Manchester City
intensified. Watching his heroes play at the
Etihad Stadium was an experience he cherished.
He dreamed of one day stepping onto that same
pitch, not as a fan but as a player.

But dreams alone weren't enough. Phil knew
that to achieve his goals, he would have to work
harder than ever. His early years in Stockport
were a time of discovery, growth, and
preparation for the challenges ahead.

Phil Foden's childhood in Stockport wasn't just
the beginning of his journey—it was the
foundation upon which he built his extraordinary
career. Surrounded by a supportive family,
inspired by a football-loving community, and

driven by an unshakable passion for the game, Phil took his first steps toward greatness in this small but vibrant town.

This chapter is not just about Phil's early life; it's a reminder that greatness often begins in the most ordinary places. It's a testament to the power of dreams, hard work, and the support of loved ones. As we continue to explore Phil's story, we'll see how these early influences shaped him into the football star he is today.

CHAPTER 2: DISCOVERING A PASSION FOR FOOTBALL

Phil Foden's love for football wasn't something that developed overnight—it was a bond that grew stronger with every kick of the ball. In Stockport, the streets, parks, and playgrounds became his first training grounds. For Phil, football wasn't just a hobby; it was his world, a place where he felt truly free and alive.

From the moment he could walk, Phil seemed destined to play football. His parents often shared stories of how little Phil would kick anything that resembled a ball around the house. Whether it was a rolled-up pair of socks or a tennis ball, Phil's feet always seemed to find a way to dribble it.

A Lifelong Love Begins

Phil's first encounters with organized football came when he joined local youth teams. Even at a young age, his natural talent was apparent. Coaches were amazed by his ability to control the ball, his sharp instincts on the field, and his sheer determination to win. Phil wasn't just playing for fun; he was playing because he loved the game with all his heart.

He idolized players from Manchester City and often tried to mimic their moves. Watching live matches or highlights, Phil would study how professional players dribbled, passed, and scored. Then, he would head outside to practice those very moves, imagining himself in their shoes.

The Magic of the Playground

For Phil, the playground was more than just a place to play—it was his first arena. He would gather his friends for impromptu matches, often leading his team to victory with dazzling footwork and clever strategies. These games weren't about trophies or recognition; they were about pure, unfiltered joy.

Even when playing against older kids, Phil never backed down. His fearless attitude and competitive spirit earned him respect, and he quickly became the kid everyone wanted on their team.

Early Influences and Role Models

Every great athlete has role models, and Phil was no exception. He looked up to players like David Silva and Sergio Agüero, both legends at Manchester City. Their skills and dedication inspired Phil to dream bigger and push himself harder.

But Phil's biggest inspiration came closer to home—his family. His father, a lifelong Manchester City supporter, often played football with Phil in their backyard. These moments weren't just fun; they were lessons in discipline, teamwork, and perseverance.

Small Steps, Big Dreams

Phil's passion for football grew with every passing day. He began participating in more local tournaments, where his talent was undeniable. Coaches and scouts started to take notice of the young boy with incredible skills and an infectious love for the game.

Despite the growing attention, Phil remained grounded. He didn't play for fame or praise; he played because he couldn't imagine life without football. It was his escape, his joy, and his dream all rolled into one.

The Support That Made It Possible

Behind every young talent is a support system, and Phil's family played a crucial role in nurturing his passion. His parents worked hard to ensure he had everything he needed, from proper gear to transportation for games. They believed in his dream as much as he did, often sacrificing their own needs to help him succeed.

Phil's coaches also played an essential role in shaping his early years. They not only taught him the technical aspects of the game but also instilled in him the importance of teamwork, discipline, and sportsmanship.

The Beginning of Something Special

Phil's journey in football was still in its early stages, but it was clear to everyone around him that he was destined for greatness. His passion, combined with his talent and the unwavering support of his family, set the stage for what would become an extraordinary career.

As we move to the next chapter, we'll follow Phil's journey from the playgrounds of Stockport to one of the best football academies in the world. It's a story of dreams, dedication, and the belief that anything is possible when you truly love what you do.

CHAPTER 3: JOINING MANCHESTER CITY'S ACADEMY

Phil Foden's journey from the streets of Stockport to Manchester City's prestigious academy is a story of dreams coming true, determination, and unwavering support. Joining the academy marked a turning point in Phil's life, where his passion for football transitioned into a structured pathway toward professional greatness.

A Boy with Big Dreams

From a young age, Phil had been a dedicated Manchester City fan. Supporting the club was a family tradition, with his father taking him to watch games at the Etihad Stadium. For Phil, wearing the Manchester City shirt was more than a dream—it was an ultimate goal. His love for the team and his extraordinary skills on the pitch made him stand out in local youth leagues.

Scouts from Manchester City's academy first noticed Phil when he was just eight years old. His agility, quick decision-making, and ability to control the ball in tight spaces amazed them. They saw something special in this young boy from Stockport—a raw talent that could be nurtured into something extraordinary.

The Call That Changed Everything
The day Phil was invited to join Manchester City's academy was unforgettable. His family celebrated the news, knowing how much it

meant to him. While Phil was thrilled, he also understood that joining the academy was just the beginning. It wasn't just about talent; it was about hard work, discipline, and a willingness to learn.

A New World of Football

Manchester City's academy wasn't like anything Phil had experienced before. It was a place where some of the best young talents from across the region trained together, each with dreams of becoming professional footballers. The facilities were state-of-the-art, with top-tier coaches, training programs, and resources designed to develop future stars.

For Phil, it was like stepping into a dream. Every day was an opportunity to improve, and he eagerly soaked up everything he could. The academy emphasized not only technical skills but also teamwork, strategy, and mental strength. Phil learned to balance his natural flair with tactical discipline, becoming a more complete player.

Balancing School and Football
One of the biggest challenges Phil faced was balancing his schoolwork with his commitment to the academy. Training sessions were intense and frequent, often leaving little time for anything else. However, Phil's parents and coaches made sure he stayed on top of his studies.

Phil's family emphasized the importance of education, knowing that football, while promising, could be unpredictable. With their support, Phil managed to excel both on the pitch and in the classroom. He often spent his evenings catching up on homework after training, demonstrating a level of discipline and maturity beyond his years.

Learning from the Best

At the academy, Phil had the chance to interact with some of the best coaches in the game. They recognized his potential and pushed him to achieve more. Training sessions were designed to challenge him, forcing him to think faster, move smarter, and play harder.

Phil also had the privilege of watching Manchester City's first team train occasionally. Seeing his idols up close inspired him to work even harder. He dreamed of the day he would share the pitch with them, wearing the same iconic blue jersey.

Challenges and Sacrifices

The road to success was not without its challenges. Phil had to make significant sacrifices, often missing out on time with friends and family. While his peers were enjoying typical childhood activities, Phil was dedicating himself to football.

There were moments of doubt, as is natural for any young athlete. Intense training schedules, high expectations, and the pressure to perform could be overwhelming. However, Phil's love for the game and the unwavering support of his family kept him going.

Rising Through the Academy Ranks

As the years went by, Phil continued to impress everyone at the academy. His technical skills, vision, and determination set him apart from his peers. He quickly rose through the ranks, becoming a key player in his age group.

Phil's performances in youth tournaments were particularly notable. He often led his team to victory, displaying leadership qualities that hinted at his future as a star player. Coaches praised not only his talent but also his humility and work ethic.

A Dream Taking Shape

By the time Phil reached his teenage years, it was clear that he was on the path to something special. Manchester City's academy had provided him with the tools, training, and experience needed to take his game to the next level.

Phil's journey at the academy wasn't just about becoming a better player; it was about growing as a person. He learned the values of discipline, teamwork, and perseverance—lessons that would serve him well in his professional career.

Looking Ahead

Joining Manchester City's academy was the first major step in Phil Foden's journey to football stardom. It was a place where his dreams began to take shape, and his potential started to shine.

In the next chapter, we'll explore how Phil's hard work and dedication helped him overcome challenges and continue his rise through the ranks. It's a story of resilience, passion, and the relentless pursuit of a dream.

CHAPTER 4: HARD WORK AND DEDICATION

Phil Foden's journey from a promising academy player to a professional footballer is a testament to the power of hard work and dedication. While talent may open doors, it's the perseverance and effort behind the scenes that truly shape a star. Phil's story during this stage of his life is filled with challenges, sacrifices, and moments of triumph, all driven by his unyielding determination to succeed.

Early Challenges

Life at Manchester City's academy was far from easy. The competition was fierce, with every young player striving to prove themselves. For

Phil, standing out required more than just his natural ability. He needed to constantly improve, adapt, and show that he deserved his place.

Training sessions were grueling, often stretching his physical and mental limits. Phil had to refine every aspect of his game, from his ball control and passing accuracy to his stamina and decision-making under pressure. It was a steep learning curve, but Phil embraced the challenge with enthusiasm and grit.

The Importance of Routine

Phil understood early on that consistency was key to achieving his goals. He developed a daily routine that balanced rigorous training with proper rest, nutrition, and schoolwork. His disciplined lifestyle became the foundation for his progress.

Mornings often began with fitness drills, focusing on building strength and endurance. Afternoons were dedicated to tactical training, where he honed his understanding of the game. In the evenings, Phil would analyze his performance, identifying areas for improvement.

Support from Family and Coaches
Phil's journey was supported by a strong network of people who believed in him. His family remained his biggest cheerleaders, encouraging him to keep going even when the going got tough. They often reminded him of how far he had come and how much further he could go with persistence.

The coaches at Manchester City also played a pivotal role. They pushed Phil to strive for excellence, offering guidance and constructive feedback. While they were demanding, they also provided the mentorship needed to help him grow.

Overcoming Setbacks

Every athlete faces setbacks, and Phil was no exception. Whether it was losing a crucial match, dealing with minor injuries, or navigating the pressures of balancing football and school, these moments tested his resolve.

Instead of letting setbacks discourage him, Phil used them as opportunities to learn and grow. Each challenge became a stepping stone, strengthening his character and determination. He began to view obstacles not as barriers but as opportunities to prove himself.

Staying Focused

One of Phil's most remarkable traits was his ability to stay focused on his goals. While many young players could get distracted by the excitement of being part of a prestigious academy, Phil remained grounded.

He avoided distractions and kept his eyes on the bigger picture. His coaches often praised him for his maturity, noting that he never let success get to his head. Phil understood that the journey to the top required patience, persistence, and humility.

Sacrifices Along the Way

Phil's dedication came with sacrifices. He missed out on many typical teenage experiences, such as spending time with friends or going on family vacations. Instead, he poured his energy into training and self-improvement.

While these sacrifices weren't easy, Phil never regretted them. He knew that every hour spent on the pitch brought him closer to achieving his dream. His love for football made the sacrifices worthwhile.

Moments of Breakthrough

Phil's hard work began to pay off in remarkable ways. His performances in youth tournaments and training sessions consistently impressed his coaches. He became known for his vision, creativity, and ability to stay calm under pressure.

One of his standout moments was scoring a winning goal during a critical academy match.

That goal not only secured victory for his team but also highlighted Phil's ability to perform in high-stakes situations. Moments like these fueled his confidence and reinforced his belief in his abilities.

Learning from Role Models

During this period, Phil closely observed Manchester City's senior players. He admired their skill, professionalism, and dedication to the game. Players like David Silva and Kevin De Bruyne became his inspirations, showing him what it meant to be a world-class footballer.

Phil often tried to emulate their qualities, both on and off the pitch. Their success stories motivated him to push harder, knowing that he could one day follow in their footsteps.

The Turning Point

By the time Phil was in his mid-teens, his relentless dedication began to set him apart from his peers. His coaches saw in him a player who wasn't just talented but also hard working and mentally tough.

This recognition marked a turning point in Phil's journey. He was no longer just another academy player; he was a rising star with the potential to make it to the professional stage.

A Lesson in Perseverance

Phil Foden's story during this phase of his life is a powerful lesson in perseverance. It shows that talent alone isn't enough; it's the effort and dedication behind the scenes that truly define success.

Phil's commitment to his craft laid the foundation for his future achievements. In the next chapter, we'll explore how his hard work paid off as he rose through the ranks to join Manchester City's first team—a dream that was finally coming true.

CHAPTER 5: RISING THROUGH THE RANKS

After years of hard work and dedication at Manchester City's academy, Phil Foden's big break was finally on the horizon. His rise through the ranks of the club's youth teams wasn't just a matter of talent—it was a story of persistence, confidence, and the unwavering belief that his dream of playing for Manchester City's first team could become a reality.

A Step Closer to His Dream
By the time Phil turned 16, he was already a standout player in the academy, catching the eye of Manchester City's top coaches. His technical ability, vision, and maturity on the field made

him an obvious candidate for promotion to the first team. However, stepping up from the youth academy to playing professionally was no small feat.

At this stage, Phil had to prove himself against older, more experienced players—some of whom had already made their names in top leagues around the world. The competition was fierce, but Phil's talent and relentless work ethic ensured that he was ready for the challenge.

Training with the First Team
The moment Phil was invited to train with Manchester City's first team was a huge milestone in his career. It was the opportunity he had dreamed of for years, and he didn't take it lightly.

Training with world-class players like Sergio Agüero, Raheem Sterling, and Kevin De Bruyne was a surreal experience for Phil. He was now learning from some of the best footballers in the world, watching how they approached every drill, how they analyzed the game, and how they maintained their high level of performance.

Phil found himself inspired by the senior players' professionalism and passion for the game. He quickly adapted to the pace of training, constantly pushing himself to meet the high standards expected at such an elite level. His eagerness to learn and improve stood out, earning him the respect of both coaches and players.

A Debut to Remember

Phil's big moment arrived in 2016, when he made his debut for Manchester City's first team in a Champions League match against Feyenoord. At just 17 years old, he became one of the youngest players in the club's history to feature in a senior match.

The debut was a dream come true for Phil. It was the culmination of years of hard work, sacrifice, and perseverance. But despite the excitement, Phil remained humble. He knew that his journey had just begun, and he was determined to make the most of the opportunity.

Overcoming Doubts

As with any young player stepping up to the senior team, there were moments of self-doubt. Phil was now playing with world-class talent, and the pressure to perform was immense. But instead of letting these challenges overwhelm him, he used them as motivation.

In fact, Phil's calmness under pressure became one of his trademarks. Whether he was playing in a high-stakes game or training alongside football legends, he never let the moment get too big for him. His focus and composure on the ball made him stand out, even in the most intense situations.

Earning Pep Guardiola's Trust

Phil's rise through the ranks was accelerated by the trust that Manchester City's manager, Pep Guardiola, placed in him. Guardiola recognized Phil's potential and was quick to give him important opportunities.

Guardiola's coaching philosophy was all about technical skill, fast-paced play, and fluidity on the field—qualities that aligned perfectly with Phil's style of play. The manager often praised Phil's ability to make quick, smart decisions under pressure and his natural football intelligence.

Under Guardiola's guidance, Phil's game reached new heights. Guardiola encouraged him to express himself on the pitch, to take risks, and to never shy away from the challenge. With the manager's support, Phil's confidence grew, and he continued to excel in every game he played.

Key Moments in His Rise
Phil's early appearances for Manchester City were filled with memorable moments that showcased his abilities. His performances in the

League Cup and domestic league matches were impressive, as he quickly became known for his quick footwork, creativity, and ability to make key contributions to his team's success.

One of his standout performances came in a League Cup match against Oxford United in 2018. Phil scored two goals and provided an assist, showing his skill, vision, and maturity. The match was a clear sign that he had arrived as a serious contender for a regular spot in the first team.

Phil's Role in Manchester City's Success
As Phil's career progressed, he became a key player in Manchester City's attack. His vision, passing range, and technical ability made him a valuable asset for the team. He also became known for his versatility, able to play in several

attacking positions, from central midfield to winger.

Phil's contributions were vital to Manchester City's success in both domestic and international competitions. His performances helped the team win multiple Premier League titles, FA Cups, and League Cups. Each victory was a reflection of the hard work and determination that had taken Phil from the academy to the top of English football.

Overcoming Setbacks
While Phil's rise was fast and impressive, it wasn't without setbacks. There were times when he faced stiff competition for a starting spot, or when his performances didn't meet the high standards he had set for himself.

However, Phil's resilience and willingness to learn from each setback were key factors in his continued success. He understood that the road to becoming a top footballer was filled with challenges, and instead of shying away from them, he faced them head-on, using each experience to grow stronger.

Recognition and Praise
As Phil's career flourished, his efforts began to receive widespread recognition. His performances for Manchester City caught the attention of football fans, pundits, and former players alike. He became known as one of the brightest young talents in world football.

Phil's rise was also celebrated by his teammates, who admired his skill, work ethic, and attitude. He quickly became a key figure in Manchester

City's locker room, a player everyone could count on in big moments.

Looking Toward the Future

By the time Phil Foden had secured his place in Manchester City's first team, he had already accomplished so much. But for him, the journey was far from over. Phil knew that to stay at the top, he had to continue working hard, improving his skills, and pushing himself to new heights.

Phil's rise through the ranks was a reminder that dreams don't come true overnight—they take time, effort, and a lot of hard work. His journey from the academy to the first team was proof that dedication, resilience, and passion are key ingredients to success in any field.

Phil foden

In the next chapter, we'll take a closer look at Phil Foden's impact at Manchester City—his moments of brilliance, his unforgettable performances, and the legacy he's starting to build at one of the world's top football clubs.

CHAPTER 6: THE MAGIC OF PLAYING FOR MANCHESTER CITY

Phil Foden had made it. He had worked tirelessly for years, overcoming countless obstacles, and now he was playing for one of the best football clubs in the world: Manchester City. The bright lights of the Etihad Stadium, the cheers of thousands of fans, and the thrill of playing alongside the best players in the world—it was a dream come true for Phil. But as exciting as it was, this was just the beginning of a new chapter in his football career.

A Dream Debut

Phil Foden's first appearance in a competitive match for Manchester City came in 2017, when he was just 17 years old. He stepped onto the pitch in a Champions League match, a game that was watched by millions of people across the world. This moment was the culmination of years of hard work, training, and sacrifices. Phil had dreamed of playing in these big matches ever since he was a little boy, and now, here he was, playing for one of the biggest clubs in Europe.

His debut was not only a moment of personal achievement but also a reflection of the faith that manager Pep Guardiola had in him. Guardiola had been watching Phil's progress and saw something special in the young player. He believed Phil was ready to make his mark on the team.

From that moment, Phil's career at Manchester City began to soar. His potential was clear for all to see—he was fast, clever, and showed a maturity on the ball that was rare for someone his age. Even though he was young, Phil proved that he belonged on the biggest stage, and he quickly became a key player for City.

The Rise of a Young Star

It didn't take long for Phil to establish himself as one of Manchester City's brightest young talents. His versatility on the field was one of his greatest strengths. He could play in various positions—whether in central midfield, as a winger, or even as a forward. His ability to adapt to different roles made him an invaluable player for City, as he could step into whichever position the team needed him most.

One of the things that set Phil apart was his creativity. He had an incredible vision of the game. His quick thinking allowed him to make key passes, create chances, and break through opposition defenses with ease. Phil's football intelligence and decision-making on the pitch were beyond his years, and it didn't take long for fans and analysts alike to notice that he had the potential to become one of the best in the world.

One of the most magical moments of Phil's early career with Manchester City came in the 2018-2019 season. In the Carabao Cup final against Chelsea, Phil delivered a brilliant performance that earned him widespread recognition. He scored his first senior goal for City in that match, helping his team win the trophy. His joy and excitement were clear to see,

and it was a sign of the many great moments still
to come.

A Key Player in Manchester City's Success
Phil's growth at Manchester City didn't stop
with just one memorable goal. As the seasons
went on, he became an essential part of the team.
Under the guidance of Pep Guardiola, Phil
flourished, becoming one of the team's most
important and exciting players.

Manchester City's style of play, which focuses
on possession, quick passing, and attacking
football, suited Phil perfectly. His ability to
retain the ball, make precise passes, and create
space for others allowed him to fit seamlessly
into the team's dynamic. He was often seen
combining beautifully with teammates like
Kevin De Bruyne, Sergio Agüero, and Raheem

Sterling, each one of them helping elevate Phil's game even further.

Phil's contributions were not limited to just one area of the pitch. He would score goals, assist his teammates, and even track back to help with defensive duties. His all-around abilities made him a complete player, and it was clear that Phil was growing into a leader for the team.

Big Wins and Major Titles

As Phil continued to develop, Manchester City's success continued to grow. In the 2018-2019 season, Phil and the team won the Premier League, the FA Cup, and the Carabao Cup. These victories were a testament to Manchester City's dominance in English football, and Phil played a significant role in those triumphs.

But Phil didn't stop there. He was part of Manchester City's squad that went on to win even more titles in the years that followed. Whether it was the Premier League or the FA Cup, Phil consistently contributed with key performances that helped City reach the top of English football. His growth as a player was mirrored by Manchester City's continued success, and together, they became one of the most feared teams in Europe.

International Glory and Recognition

Phil's success at Manchester City didn't go unnoticed by the England national team. As his performances for City improved, he earned his first call-up to represent England in 2020. Phil had now reached the highest level of football, playing not only for his club but for his country too.

His debut for England was another proud moment in his young career. Phil showed his quality in international matches, helping England win important fixtures and establish themselves as one of the top teams in the world. Representing his country was a huge honor for Phil, and he was determined to make the most of every opportunity.

But Phil's rise was not just about the trophies and goals; it was about his journey to becoming a true football star. His performances in key games, his development as a player, and his ability to inspire others made him a role model for kids everywhere who dreamed of playing football.

Becoming a Role Model

Phil foden

As Phil's career flourished, he became more than just a talented footballer—he became a symbol of hard work and perseverance. His rise to success showed young people that with dedication and passion, dreams could come true. Phil's story inspired children everywhere, especially those who came from small towns like Stockport, where it seemed impossible to make it to the top.

Phil's journey was not only about his achievements on the pitch; it was also about his character. Despite his success, he remained grounded and humble, always remembering where he came from. He was dedicated to giving back to his community, supporting local projects, and showing others that hard work and good values were just as important as talent.

The Magic of Playing for Manchester City
Looking back at Phil's time at Manchester City,
it's easy to see why playing for the club has been
such a magical experience for him. He has
become part of a team that is one of the best in
the world, winning numerous titles and
achieving greatness together. But for Phil,
playing for Manchester City was not just about
winning trophies—it was about being part of
something bigger than himself, about learning
from the best, and about contributing to a team
that had a strong sense of unity and purpose.
For Phil Foden, playing for Manchester City is a
dream come true. And as his career continues to
evolve, there's no doubt that the best is yet to
come. In the next chapter, we'll take a closer
look at Phil's journey with the England national
team and how he's making a name for himself
on the international stage.

CHAPTER 7: PHIL FODEN ON THE INTERNATIONAL STAGE

Phil Foden's journey to representing his country, England, was a natural progression in his rise to stardom. After impressing with Manchester City, he had caught the attention of England's national team coaches, and soon enough, he was donning the iconic Three Lions jersey. Playing for England was the ultimate achievement for Phil, a young boy who had always dreamed of playing on the world's biggest football stages.

Earning His First England Call-Up

In 2020, after several outstanding performances for Manchester City, Phil Foden received his first call-up to the England national team. This was a huge moment in his career. The call-up was not just a recognition of his talent but also an acknowledgment of his potential to play at the highest level. For a boy who grew up in Stockport, playing for his country was the culmination of a childhood dream.

Phil's first appearance for England came in a UEFA Nations League match against Iceland in September 2020. At just 20 years old, he was already playing alongside some of the best footballers in the world, including Harry Kane, Raheem Sterling, and Jordan Henderson. It was a moment of immense pride for Phil and his family, as they saw the young boy who once kicked a ball around in the streets of Stockport now representing his country on the international stage.

Gaining International Experience

After his debut, Phil quickly became a regular member of the England squad. His performances for Manchester City had shown that he had the quality to play against some of the best teams in the world, and he brought that same energy to the international level. Whether playing in friendly matches or competitive fixtures, Phil displayed the same creativity, intelligence, and skill that had made him a star at Manchester City.

One of Phil's standout performances for England came during the Euro 2020 tournament, which took place in 2021 due to the COVID-19 pandemic. The competition was a massive event, with teams from all over Europe competing for glory. Phil Foden was part of England's squad, and he quickly became one of the key players. His dazzling footwork, eye for a pass, and ability to change the game were on full display, and England fans began to see the potential of having a player like Phil on their team.

Though England's journey in the tournament was not without challenges, Phil proved himself to be an invaluable asset, playing in critical matches and helping his team reach the final. Even though England fell short in the final against Italy, it was clear that Phil had already established himself as one of the brightest young stars in international football.

A Key Figure in England's Future

Phil's growth continued as he gained more international experience. He was becoming more comfortable in the international spotlight, and with every game, he was improving and gaining more confidence. Phil's ability to perform under pressure showed that he was ready for the big moments, and that's exactly what England needed—someone who could step up when it mattered the most.

England's head coach, Gareth Southgate, was impressed by Phil's maturity and his ability to handle the responsibility of playing for his country. Southgate often praised Phil for his dedication, work ethic, and his willingness to learn. For Southgate, Phil was not just a talented player; he was a player with a bright future who could play a significant role in England's success for years to come.

Phil's time with England continued to grow in importance. He became a regular starter in England's World Cup qualifiers and other international competitions, contributing to their strong performances. His partnership with other young stars like Harry Kane and Bukayo Saka created a dynamic and exciting team that was capable of competing with the best in the world.

The England Journey Continues

As Phil Foden continues to represent England, his journey is just beginning. He has already achieved so much, but there is still so much more to come. Phil is now a key player in England's national team, and his contributions will be crucial in the coming years, especially as England targets success in future international tournaments like the FIFA World Cup and the UEFA European Championship.

Phil's journey with the national team is an inspiration for young footballers everywhere. His story shows that with talent, hard work, and the right mindset, it is possible to represent your country at the highest level. For Phil, playing for England is not just about wearing the national jersey; it's about making his country proud and giving everything for the team.

Representing England with Pride

Playing for your country is one of the highest honors a footballer can achieve. For Phil Foden, representing England is not just a career milestone; it's a source of immense pride. Every time he steps onto the pitch wearing the England jersey, he is representing not just himself but also his family, his hometown, and the millions of England fans who support the national team.

Phil's passion for playing for England is clear. It's not just about the fame or the recognition; it's about playing for something bigger than himself. He is playing for his country and for the future of English football. And with Phil Foden in the squad, England fans have a lot to look forward to in the years ahead.

In the next chapter, we will look at the people who inspired Phil Foden along the way. From family members to football idols, these role models played a significant part in shaping the young star we know today.

CHAPTER 8: ROLE MODELS AND INSPIRATIONS

Phil Foden's journey to becoming a football superstar was not one he took alone. Along the way, he was influenced and motivated by various role models, both on and off the pitch. These figures helped shape his approach to the game, his work ethic, and his attitude towards life. In this chapter, we'll explore the people who inspired Phil, and how he, in turn, has become an inspiration to others.

A Family That Always Believed in Him
Phil's first and perhaps most important role models were his family. From a young age, Phil's parents, Clare and Phil Foden Sr.,

provided him with the love, support, and encouragement he needed to chase his dreams. They made sure that Phil had every opportunity to succeed, whether it was through providing him with the resources to play football or attending his matches to cheer him on.

Phil's family has always been a constant source of motivation for him. His mother, Clare, has often spoken about how proud she is of her son and how she always knew he had the talent to make it big. She and his father were there for him every step of the way, from his early days at Stockport County to his rise through Manchester City's youth academy. Their belief in him gave Phil the confidence to continue pursuing his dream, even when the journey got tough.

Phil has often spoken about how much his family means to him and how they have kept him grounded throughout his rise to fame. In the competitive world of football, it can be easy to lose sight of what really matters, but Phil's family has always reminded him of where he came from and the values that are important to him. They have been his biggest supporters and have shaped the humble, hard working person he is today.

The Influence of Football Legends
In addition to his family, Phil was inspired by some of the greatest footballers to ever play the game. Like many young boys, Phil grew up idolizing football stars. However, it was not just their skills on the field that he admired; it was their dedication, passion, and commitment to the game that resonated with him.

One of Phil's biggest footballing inspirations was Barcelona legend Lionel Messi. Messi, often regarded as one of the greatest players of all time, was a player that Phil looked up to throughout his childhood. The Argentine forward's incredible dribbling skills, vision, and ability to score from almost any position on the field made him a role model for aspiring footballers like Phil. Messi's success at Barcelona and his ability to maintain his level of excellence year after year taught Phil the importance of consistency and always striving for greatness.

Another major influence on Phil was Manchester City's own David Silva. Silva, a creative midfielder known for his dazzling skills and playmaking ability, became one of Phil's key role models. As a young player coming up through the ranks at Manchester City, Phil had the opportunity to watch Silva closely and learn from him. Silva's ability to control the game with his passing, his vision, and his technique was something Phil admired greatly, and he has often mentioned how much he learned from the Spanish star. Silva's calm and composed style of play served as an example for Phil to follow, and he aspired to incorporate similar qualities into his own game.

As Phil's career progressed, he also looked up to other English footballing legends like Steven Gerrard and Frank Lampard. These two midfield maestros were not only great players but also leaders who played key roles in both club and international football. Their work ethic, leadership qualities, and ability to perform in big moments showed Phil the importance of being a complete player, someone who can both inspire teammates and take responsibility when needed.

The Influence of Pep Guardiola
One of the most significant influences on Phil's career has been his manager at Manchester City, Pep Guardiola. Guardiola, one of the most successful and respected managers in football, has played a crucial role in developing Phil's game. When Guardiola arrived at Manchester City in 2016, he brought with him a philosophy of possession-based football that emphasized quick passing, movement, and creativity. For a young player like Phil, who was already known for his flair and skill, Guardiola's methods were the perfect fit.

Guardiola's faith in Phil has been a key part of his development. The Spanish manager was quick to recognize Phil's potential and gave him opportunities to play in Manchester City's first team, despite his young age. Guardiola has often praised Phil for his intelligence, work ethic, and ability to make an impact on the pitch. Under Guardiola's guidance, Phil has grown into one of the most promising young talents in world football.

What's more, Guardiola has helped Phil develop a deeper understanding of the game, pushing him to become not just a skilful player but also a smart one. Guardiola's attention to detail, tactical awareness, and emphasis on team play have been invaluable lessons for Phil. As he continues to work with one of the greatest managers of all time, Phil has the chance to learn and grow, both as a player and as a person.

Becoming an Inspiration for Others
While Phil Foden has had many role models throughout his life, he has also become an inspiration to others. Young footballers all over the world look up to Phil as a symbol of what can be achieved through hard work and determination. His story of growing up in Stockport, rising through Manchester City's academy, and becoming one of the best players in the world is one that resonates with kids who dream of playing professional football.

Phil's humility and work ethic have made him a role model for young athletes. He is proof that with the right mindset, anything is possible. Despite his success, Phil has remained grounded,

always remembering his roots and the people
who helped him along the way. He shows young
footballers that talent alone is not enough to
make it to the top; it takes discipline,
commitment, and a willingness to learn from
others.

Phil is also becoming an inspiration off the field.
He uses his platform to encourage young people
to chase their dreams and never give up.
Whether through social media or interviews, Phil
often shares messages of motivation and
positivity, reminding kids that with hard work
and a positive attitude, anything is possible.
In the next chapter, we will look at the important
life lessons that can be learned from Phil
Foden's journey. From dreaming big to
overcoming challenges, Phil's story is full of
valuable lessons for young readers everywhere.

CHAPTER 9: LESSONS FROM PHIL FODEN'S JOURNEY

Phil Foden's story is more than just about football; it's a powerful tale of perseverance, hard work, and believing in your dreams. From growing up in Stockport to becoming one of the best young footballers in the world, Phil's journey teaches us many important life lessons. In this chapter, we'll explore the key lessons we can all learn from his experiences, both on and off the pitch.

1. Dream Big and Never Stop Believing

Phil foden

One of the most important lessons from Phil's journey is the power of dreaming big. When Phil was a child, he dreamed of becoming a professional footballer. Many people told him it was a long shot, but Phil never gave up on his dream. He worked hard every day, focused on his goal, and believed in himself, even when things got tough.

Phil's story shows us that if you have a dream, no matter how big it seems, you should never stop believing in it. It's easy to get discouraged, but Phil's success teaches us that anything is possible if we stay committed to our goals and keep pushing forward. Whether you want to become a footballer, a scientist, an artist, or anything else, having a big dream is the first step toward success.

2. Hard Work Pays Off

Phil didn't just dream about becoming a footballer; he worked incredibly hard to make that dream a reality. From a young age, he was training, practicing, and improving his skills. He didn't just rely on his natural talent; he put in the effort to become the best player he could be.

In his journey, Phil faced many challenges, but instead of giving up, he used each obstacle as an opportunity to grow. Whether it was competing against older, more experienced players or dealing with setbacks, Phil remained focused and dedicated. His story teaches us that hard work is key to success. No matter what challenges you face, if you keep working hard and never give up, you will get closer to reaching your dreams.

3. Embrace the Support of Others

No one achieves success alone, and Phil Foden is a great example of this. While Phil worked hard, he was also supported by his family, coaches, and teammates along the way. His parents, Clare and Phil Sr., always believed in him and were there to encourage him. His coaches at Stockport County and Manchester City saw his potential and helped him develop his skills.

Phil's story reminds us that it's important to embrace the support of others. Whether it's your family, friends, teachers, or coaches, having people who believe in you can make all the difference. You don't have to do everything on your own. Accepting help and learning from those around you can help you grow and succeed.

4. Learn from Your Mistakes and Keep
Improving

No one is perfect, and Phil Foden's journey was
filled with mistakes and setbacks. But instead of
letting these mistakes stop him, Phil learned
from them and kept improving. Whether it was
making a mistake in a match or being told he
wasn't ready for the first team, Phil took those
moments as opportunities to learn and get better.

This lesson is important for everyone. No matter
what we do in life, we will make mistakes. The
key is to not give up or get discouraged. Instead,
we should learn from those mistakes, work to
improve, and keep going. Just like Phil, we can
always grow and get better, no matter how many
times we stumble along the way.

5. Be Humble, No Matter How Successful You Are

Despite his success and fame, Phil Foden has remained humble. He hasn't let his accomplishments go to his head, and he still values hard work and teamwork over individual glory. He always credits his teammates and coaches for helping him succeed, showing that no one achieves greatness alone.

Phil's humility is an important lesson for all of us. Success is not just about being the best; it's about staying grounded and respecting others along the way. Whether you're the best player on your team or you've achieved something great in your life, it's important to remember where you came from and stay humble. Phil's example shows us that true greatness isn't just about talent; it's also about kindness, respect, and staying true to who you are.

6. Focus on the Bigger Picture

Throughout his career, Phil has shown that he doesn't just focus on individual glory but on the success of his team. Whether it's scoring goals, making assists, or working hard to support his teammates, Phil understands that football is a team game. He knows that a team's success is more important than individual achievements.

This lesson is valuable in many areas of life. While it's important to strive for personal success, it's equally important to remember that we are part of a bigger picture. Whether it's in sports, school, or work, being a team player and supporting those around you can lead to greater success for everyone involved. By focusing on the bigger picture, we can all contribute to making things better for ourselves and others.

7. Enjoy the Journey, Not Just the Destination
While Phil has achieved so much in his young career, he's always emphasized the importance of enjoying the journey. He loves playing football, and he enjoys every moment of being on the pitch, whether it's a big match or a small training session. For Phil, the love of the game is what keeps him motivated, not just the trophies and titles.

This is an important lesson for all of us. It's easy to get caught up in thinking about the end goal, but enjoying the process along the way makes the journey much more fulfilling. Whether you're working towards a big goal or just doing something you love, taking the time to enjoy the experience can make everything more rewarding.

8. Never Stop Learning

Phil has always been someone who loves to learn and improve. Even as one of the top young players in the world, he continues to push himself to learn new skills and techniques. His dedication to self-improvement is one of the reasons why he continues to get better every year.

This lesson teaches us the importance of continuous learning. No matter how old we are or how much we know, there's always room to grow and improve. Whether it's in football, school, or any other area of life, being open to learning new things can help us become better at what we do and reach our full potential.

FUN FACTS ABOUT PHIL FODEN

Phil Foden is known for his incredible skills on the football pitch, but there's much more to him than just his performances on game day. In this chapter, we'll explore some fun and surprising facts about Phil Foden's life, both on and off the field. These facts will give you a better understanding of who Phil is as a person, beyond the famous football star.

1. Phil Was a Manchester City Fan Before Joining the Club

Before he even kicked a ball for Manchester City, Phil Foden was a huge fan of the club.

Growing up in Stockport, a town just outside Manchester, he watched City matches with his family and dreamt of one day playing for the team. His father, Phil Sr., also supported Manchester City, so Phil's love for the club was passed down through the family.

It's a dream come true for Phil to play for the team he supported as a child. His story is a perfect example of how dreams can come true when you put in the effort and stay focused on your goals. Being a fan of the club gave him extra motivation to work hard, knowing that one day he could represent Manchester City on the world stage.

2. Phil Was a Multi-Sport Athlete Growing Up

Phil foden

While Phil is now known for his football talent, he wasn't always just focused on football. As a child, he played other sports like basketball and rugby. He loved staying active and trying different things, which helped him develop his skills and fitness. Playing multiple sports also gave him a competitive edge in football, as it helped improve his agility, coordination, and teamwork.

Phil's experience as a multi-sport athlete shows that trying different activities can be beneficial, even for future footballers. Sometimes, exploring other interests can help you discover new talents and ways to improve in your main sport. Whether you want to be a footballer, tennis player, or swimmer, trying new things can always teach you valuable lessons.

3. Phil's Nickname Is "The Stockport Iniesta"

When Phil was a young player at the Manchester City Academy, coaches and teammates began calling him "The Stockport Iniesta," a nod to Spanish football legend Andrés Iniesta. Iniesta is known for his incredible dribbling, vision, and passing, and Phil's style of play reminded many people of the famous midfielder.

Phil's dribbling skills, his ability to read the game, and his creative playmaking abilities are some of the qualities that earned him this nickname. While it's an honor to be compared to one of the best midfielders in football history, Phil remains humble and continues to focus on developing his own unique style of play.

4. He Made His Premier League Debut at Just 17 Years Old

Phil Foden made his Premier League debut for Manchester City at the age of just 17, which is an incredible achievement. At such a young age, many players are still playing in youth leagues or getting experience on loan to smaller clubs, but Phil was already trusted to play for one of the biggest football clubs in the world.

His debut came during the 2017-2018 season, when Manchester City's manager, Pep Guardiola, gave him a chance to show what he could do. Phil didn't waste the opportunity—he showcased his talent and skill, proving that he was ready to compete at the highest level.

Making his Premier League debut at 17 is a reminder that age doesn't always determine success. With hard work and dedication, even the youngest players can achieve big things. Phil's story shows that you can achieve your dreams at any age if you put in the effort and seize the opportunities that come your way.

5. Phil Is Known for His Humility and Work Ethic

Despite being one of the most talented young players in the world, Phil Foden is known for his humility and hard work. He doesn't let his fame or success go to his head. Instead, he stays focused on improving every day and always listens to his coaches and teammates.

Phil's attitude and work ethic have earned him respect from his teammates and coaches. They admire his willingness to learn and always give 100% on the pitch. Whether he's training or playing in a match, Phil gives his best effort every time. His dedication to improving himself is one of the reasons why he continues to grow as a player, and it's a lesson for all of us to stay humble and keep working hard, no matter how successful we become.

6. Phil Foden Is a Fan of Video Games

Like many young people, Phil Foden enjoys playing video games in his spare time. He has mentioned in interviews that he loves to relax and unwind by playing games with his friends. Football might be his main passion, but Phil is just like any other teenager when it comes to enjoying a bit of downtime.

This fun fact reminds us that it's important to have hobbies and interests outside of our main goals. Whether it's playing video games, reading, or spending time with friends, having fun and relaxing is a key part of staying balanced and motivated. Even professional athletes like Phil need time to enjoy themselves and recharge.

7. Phil Is Very Close with His Family

Phil Foden's family has always played a big role in his life and career. He is very close with his parents, Clare and Phil Sr., and his brother, who have supported him throughout his journey. Phil often talks about how important his family's support is to him and how they have helped him

stay grounded, even as he becomes more
successful.

His parents have been there for him every step of
the way, attending games, helping him stay
focused, and offering advice when needed. Phil's
relationship with his family shows how
important it is to have a strong support system,
no matter what you're trying to achieve.

8. Phil Foden Is a Role Model for Young
Footballers

Phil Foden is not just a talented player; he is also
a role model for young footballers everywhere.
His journey shows that with hard work,
dedication, and the right attitude, anyone can
achieve their dreams. Phil uses his platform to

inspire young players, encouraging them to chase their dreams and never give up.

He's also an advocate for helping others and is involved in charity work. Phil understands the importance of giving back to the community and setting a good example for younger generations. He teaches that success isn't just about being the best player; it's about being a positive influence and helping others along the way.

9. Phil Foden's Favorite Player Growing Up Was Steven Gerrard

Every player has someone they look up to, and for Phil Foden, that player was Steven Gerrard, the former captain of Liverpool and one of England's best midfielders. Growing up, Phil admired Gerrard's leadership on the pitch, his work ethic, and his ability to make a difference in big matches.

Gerrard's playing style and attitude helped shape Phil's own approach to the game. Now, Phil is following in his idol's footsteps, becoming a leader in his own right and inspiring young players around the world. It's a reminder that even the best players have role models who shape their careers and inspire them to keep improving.

10. Phil Enjoys Playing Futsal

In addition to playing traditional football, Phil Foden has a passion for futsal, a smaller version of football played on hard courts. Futsal is a fast-paced game that helps players improve their ball control, dribbling, and quick decision-making skills.

Phil's love for futsal has helped him develop many of the skills that make him such a great footballer. The tight spaces and quick thinking required in futsal translate well to the larger football pitch, allowing Phil to perform with flair and creativity. This fun fact shows that playing different versions of a sport can help athletes become even better in their main sport.

QUIZ - HOW WELL DO YOU KNOW PHIL FODEN?

Now that you've learned all about Phil Foden's incredible journey from a young dreamer in Stockport to a star at Manchester City, it's time to test your knowledge! This quiz will help you see how much you've remembered about his life and career. Ready to challenge yourself? Let's go!

1. Where is Phil Foden from?

a) London
b) Manchester
c) Stockport
d) Liverpool

Phil foden

2. At what age did Phil Foden make his debut for Manchester City's first team?

a) 16
b) 17
c) 18
d) 19

3. Which football club did Phil Foden support as a child?

a) Manchester United
b) Liverpool
c) Arsenal
d) Manchester City

4. What is the nickname given to Phil Foden because of his playing style?

Phil foden

a) The Stockport Wonder

b) The Stockport Iniesta

c) The Manchester Maestro

d) The City Star

5. Which famous footballer was Phil Foden's idol growing up?

a) Cristiano Ronaldo

b) Lionel Messi

c) Steven Gerrard

d) Wayne Rooney

6. Which sport did Phil Foden play in addition to football when he was younger?

a) Basketball

b) Rugby

Phil foden

c) Tennis

d) Cricket

7. What is Phil Foden known for being especially good at?

a) Running fast

b) Playing in defense

c) Dribbling and passing

d) Goalkeeping

8. What position does Phil Foden play for Manchester City?

a) Striker

b) Midfielder

c) Goalkeeper

d) Defender

9. What is one of Phil Foden's hobbies outside of football?

a) Painting

b) Playing video games

c) Playing the guitar

d) Swimming

10. What club did Phil Foden join when he was just a boy, helping him develop his football skills?

a) Liverpool FC Academy

b) Manchester United Academy

c) Manchester City Academy

d) Chelsea FC Academy

11. What is Phil Foden's family relationship like?

a) He's very close to his family and they've always supported him.

b) He doesn't get along with his family.

c) His family isn't interested in football.

d) He moved away from his family when he was young to focus on his career.

12. What year did Phil Foden make his Premier League debut?

a) 2015

b) 2016

c) 2017

d) 2018

13. What is the nickname Phil Foden earned due to his playing style?

Phil foden

a) The Manchester Wizard

b) The Stockport Iniesta

c) Foden the Great

d) The Little Genius

14. Which team did Phil Foden represent on the international stage?

a) England

b) Spain

c) France

d) Portugal

15. How does Phil Foden inspire other young players?

a) By showing them that hard work and dedication lead to success

b) By teaching them to focus only on winning

c) By staying away from his teammates

d) By focusing on individual success instead of the team

Answers:

1. c) Stockport

2. b) 17

3. d) Manchester City

4. b) The Stockport Iniesta

5. c) Steven Gerrard

Phil foden

6. b) Rugby

7. c) Dribbling and passing

8. b) Midfielder

9. b) Playing video games

10. c) Manchester City Academy

11. a) He's very close to his family and they've always supported him.

12. c) 2017

13. b) The Stockport Iniesta

14. a) England

15. a) By showing them that hard work and dedication lead to success

How Did You Do?

Now that you've completed the quiz, let's see how well you know Phil Foden!

Phil foden

10-15 Correct Answers: You're a Phil Foden expert! You know all about his life and career.

5-9 Correct Answers: Great job! You've learned a lot about Phil, but there's still more to discover.

0-4 Correct Answers: Don't worry, you're on your way! Keep reading and learning about Phil's amazing journey.

Whether you got all the answers right or not, remember that every player has a unique story. Phil Foden's journey shows us that anything is possible with passion, hard work, and a little bit of luck. If you keep working hard and chasing

108

your dreams, you too can make a big impact in
the world—just like Phil!

In the next chapter, we'll dive into Phil's
inspiring message for young dreamers. His
journey shows us that with perseverance and
belief in ourselves, we can accomplish amazing
things. Stay tuned for some powerful words
from Phil Foden!

PHIL'S MESSAGE TO YOUNG DREAMERS

Phil Foden's journey from Stockport to becoming a star at Manchester City is full of incredible moments, hard work, and a lot of determination. But what's even more inspiring is the message Phil has for young dreamers like you. He wants you to know that no matter where you come from or how big your dreams may seem, you can achieve anything if you believe in yourself and work hard.

Believe in Yourself

One of the most important things Phil learned as he grew up was the power of believing in himself. He knew from a young age that he wanted to play football professionally, but that dream wasn't easy to reach. There were many challenges along the way, but Phil never gave up because he truly believed that he could make it.

Even when times were tough, Phil kept pushing himself. He always worked hard, trained harder, and kept believing in his abilities. Phil wants you to know that belief in yourself is the first step to achieving anything in life. It doesn't matter if other people doubt you; as long as you believe in your own potential, you can accomplish your goals.

Work Hard Every Day

Phil Foden's success didn't come overnight. He spent years training, practicing, and improving his skills, even when no one was watching. He spent hours at the Manchester City Academy, working on his dribbling, passing, and game strategies. But it wasn't just about the physical skills. Phil also worked on his mindset, learning how to be patient, focused, and dedicated to his dream.

Phil's message to young dreamers is simple: work hard every day. Whether it's in sports, school, or any other part of life, hard work is the key to success. Every small effort you make each day brings you one step closer to reaching your goals. Phil believes that with dedication, you can turn your dreams into reality.

Stay Positive and Overcome Obstacles

As Phil's story shows, the road to success isn't always easy. There are obstacles and challenges along the way, but the important thing is how you deal with them. Phil faced many difficulties in his early years, including competing with other talented players and having to prove himself time and again. But he always stayed positive and focused on his goals.

Phil encourages you to stay positive, even when things don't go as planned. Whether you miss a goal in a game, struggle with schoolwork, or face any kind of challenge, remember that it's all part of the journey. What matters most is how you respond. Never let setbacks stop you from reaching your dreams.

Don't Be Afraid to Dream Big

Phil Foden came from a small town, but he dreamed big. He dreamed of playing for one of the best football teams in the world. He dreamed of representing his country. And today, he's doing both! But none of this would have been possible if Phil hadn't dared to dream big in the first place.

Phil wants you to know that your dreams matter. Dream as big as you want, because there's no limit to what you can achieve. Whether you want to be a footballer, an artist, a scientist, or anything else, don't be afraid to aim high. Your dreams are important, and with hard work and belief, you can achieve them.

The Importance of Teamwork

Phil foden

Although Phil Foden is often in the spotlight as a star player for Manchester City, he knows that football is a team sport. His success is not just about his individual talent, but also about how well he works with his teammates. Phil has learned the value of teamwork, trust, and supporting one another on and off the pitch.

Phil encourages young dreamers to remember that success is not always about doing everything on your own. You need to surround yourself with people who support you, who push you to be better, and who celebrate your successes with you. In life, just like in football, we all need a team. Don't be afraid to ask for help, learn from others, and give back to those who support you.

Never Stop Learning

No matter how successful you become, Phil believes that it's important to never stop learning. From his days at the Manchester City Academy to his time playing for the England national team, Phil is always looking for ways to improve. He's constantly learning new techniques, analyzing his performances, and striving to be the best player he can be.

Phil's advice to young dreamers is to always stay curious and keep learning. Every day is an opportunity to grow and get better. Whether you're learning new skills in your sport, improving your grades in school, or picking up a new hobby, never stop seeking knowledge. The more you learn, the more you'll grow.

Stay Humble and Appreciate Your Journey

Despite all of his success, Phil Foden remains humble and grateful for everything he has achieved. He understands that his journey has been shaped by his family, his coaches, and his teammates. He's never forgotten where he came from, and he values the support that's helped him along the way.

Phil's message to you is to always stay humble, no matter how far you go in life. Appreciate the people who have helped you, and never lose sight of the values that brought you to where you are. Remember, success is not just about winning or being the best—it's also about the kindness, respect, and gratitude you show to others.

Final Words of Inspiration

Phil foden

Phil Foden's story is proof that dreams do come true with hard work, dedication, and the right mindset. He started as a young boy from Stockport, with big dreams and a love for football. Today, he's one of the best young players in the world, representing both Manchester City and England. But the most important part of his story is not just his achievements—it's his journey, the lessons he learned, and the determination that kept him going.

Phil's message to you is clear: Believe in yourself, work hard every day, stay positive, and never stop chasing your dreams. No matter where you come from or what your dream is, you can achieve anything if you put your heart and mind to it. You are the only one who can shape your future, and the journey to your dreams begins today.

Remember, just like Phil Foden, you can go from being a dreamer to a doer. Keep dreaming big and working hard. The world is waiting for you to make your mark!

CONCLUSION

Phil Foden's journey is an inspiring story of hard work, perseverance, and following your dreams. From a young boy in Stockport, England, with a love for football, to becoming one of the brightest stars at Manchester City and representing his country on the international stage, Phil's success didn't happen by chance. It was the result of his dedication, belief in himself, and unwavering commitment to improving every day.

Phil's story teaches us valuable lessons about the power of dreaming big, the importance of hard work, and how we can overcome obstacles along the way. His journey shows us that no dream is too big if we are willing to put in the effort, stay focused, and never give up. Phil faced many challenges, but through it all, he kept pushing himself forward, proving that with determination, anything is possible.

As a young footballer, Phil knew that the path to success wasn't easy, but he trusted in his abilities and made the most of every opportunity. Whether it was training at Manchester City's Academy, working through tough times, or playing in front of thousands of fans, Phil always remained dedicated to his goal. His passion for football, combined with his hard work, led him to achieve great things both on and off the pitch.

But perhaps the most important lesson Phil Foden teaches is the value of staying humble and appreciating the journey. No matter how far you go or how successful you become, it's important to stay grounded, remember where you came from, and be grateful for the people who have supported you along the way.

For young dreamers, Phil's message is simple yet powerful: Believe in yourself, work hard, and never stop chasing your dreams. Whether you want to become a footballer, an artist, a scientist, or anything else, you can achieve it if you are willing to put in the effort and stay true to yourself.

Phil Foden is not just a footballer; he is a symbol of what's possible when you follow your passion, believe in your dreams, and work relentlessly to make them a reality. So, as you continue your own journey, remember that no dream is too big, and with dedication, you too can achieve greatness.

Keep pushing forward, keep dreaming big, and who knows? Maybe one day, your story will inspire the next generation of dreamers, just like Phil Foden has inspired us all.

Phil foden

Ready for more? My next book dives deeper into

BUKAYO SAKA BIOGRAPHY

Running Towards Success -

The Journey of Arsenal's Brightest Star

Stay tuned!"

Made in the USA
Coppell, TX
17 February 2025

46087012R00069